UK Ambulance Services
Emergency Response
Driver's Handbook

Class Professional Publishing

Printing history
First published 2012

The authors and publisher welcome feedback from the users of this book. Please contact the publisher:
Class Publishing Ltd,
The Exchange, Express Park, Bristol Road, Bridgwater TA6 4RR
Telephone: 01278 427843
Email: post@class.co.uk
Website: www.classprofessional.co.uk

Class Professional is an imprint of Class Publishing

A CIP catalogue record for this book is available from the British Library
ISBN 99781859593677

Designed and typeset by Typematter

Line illustrations by David Woodroffe

Printed in Slovenia by arrangement with KINT Ljubljana

Contents

Foreword

Acknowledgements

Introduction   1

  1. Law in relation to ambulance driving   2

  2. Automatic gearboxes   9

  3. Vehicle operating systems   16

  4. Principles of cornering   22

  5. Speed and safety   24

  6. Audible and visual warnings   25

  7. Lighting regulations   29

  8. Reversing and manoeuvring   31

  9. Attending motorway incidents   35

 10. Escorting vehicles   43

Appendices

Appendix 1   HDS, PTS, officer cars, BASICS Doctors   45

Appendix 2   Air Ambulance   45

Appendix 3   Highways Agency Traffic Officers   46

Appendix 4   Driving commentary   46

Appendix 5   Speed and safety/Feet travelled per second   49

Glossary   52

References   52

Foreword

The UK Ambulance Services Emergency Response Driver's Handbook is designed for ambulance personnel undertaking NHS Ambulance Service emergency response driver training.

During ambulance driver training this handbook is combined with practical instruction delivered by expert trainers.

The handbook is designed so that it can be used for self-study, either before or during a course, and for ready reference afterwards in order to maintain skill levels.

Andy Reid
Chair of Driver Training Advisory Group (DTAG)
On behalf of the NHS Ambulance Services

Acknowledgements

This handbook was initiated by the Driver Training Advisory Group, and endorsed by the Association of Ambulance Chief Executives (AACE) who are satisfied that it reflects current best practice in ambulance driver instruction. The handbook was produced in consultation with the UK NHS ambulance driver training leads.

Acknowledgements to the DTAG members of:

Northern Ireland Ambulance Service Health and Social Care Trust
Welsh Ambulance Services NHS Trust
Scottish Ambulance Service

East of England Ambulance Service NHS Trust
East Midlands Ambulance Service NHS Trust
Great Western Ambulance Service NHS Trust
London Ambulance Service NHS Trust
NHS Isle of Wight Ambulance
North East Ambulance Service NHS Foundation Trust
North West Ambulance Service NHS Trust
South Central Ambulance Service NHS Foundation Trust
South East Coast Ambulance Service NHS Foundation Trust
South Western Ambulance Service NHS Foundation Trust
West Midlands Ambulance Service NHS Trust
Yorkshire Ambulance Service NHS Trust

Special thanks to Paul Jones-Roberts of North West Ambulance Service NHS Trust who freely gave his time and expertise in the preparation of this handbook.

Introduction

This handbook provides a summary of the standards and practices expected of a driver of an ambulance service vehicle, for both emergency and non-emergency use.

It clearly identifies that technical mastery alone is insufficient to enable a driver to be safe and progressive; this has to be in conjunction with a sound knowledge of the *Highway Code, Police Roadcraft Handbook* 2007 edition, and road traffic law relating to the exemptions and non exemptions applied to emergency response driving.

More recently, there have been concerns about incidents involving emergency vehicles when responding to emergency calls. There are now increased possibilities of legal proceedings where there is evidence of unsafe, dangerous or careless driving.

No circumstances can justify contravention of any legal requirement, whether exempted or not, that would endanger lives and/or property. No emergency, no matter how serious, will justify you being involved in an accident; often mitigating circumstances are negated. Emergency vehicles being driven in any situation will attract attention, and in some cases public criticism. This is especially so when emergency warning equipment is in use. Great care and attention should be given to the manner in which you drive a service vehicle to minimise such criticism.

Law in Relation to Ambulance Driving

New guidelines on dangerous driving sentences

The Court of Appeal has issued new guideline penalties that should be considered when an incident results in death by dangerous driving and careless driving when under the influence of drink or drugs.

The Lord Chief Justice stated that, while jail terms should only be imposed where necessary: *"Normally the only appropriate sentence to an offender found guilty of these offences is a custodial sentence."*

The Court of Appeal declared that, when determining the appropriate sentence, courts should bear in mind *"how important it is to drive home the message that dangerous driving has a potentially horrific impact".*

In a summary of their lengthy guideline judgement, the three judges said: *"Drivers must know that, if a person is killed as a result of their driving dangerously, a custodial sentence will normally be imposed no matter what the mitigating circumstances."*

General driving guidelines

The Highway Code is issued with the authority of Parliament under the Road Traffic Act. Whilst failure to observe advice within the *Highway Code* does not render that person to criminal proceedings, any failure to adhere to the Code's principles, by an individual, can be used to establish or negate liability in civil or criminal proceedings.

All NHS Trust drivers should have a sound knowledge of the Highway Code. **It is a statutory obligation for all staff to maintain knowledge of the current edition of the Highway Code**. You should always drive in a manner that demonstrates to other road users their skill and knowledge of driving matters in relation to the Code.

Driving standards required by law

Every vehicle shall be driven with care and consideration for other road users. At no time must the vehicle be driven recklessly, or in a manner, or at a speed likely to cause danger to another road user (including those near to but not on the road).

Road Traffic Regulation Act 1984 s.87

Civil law

Under civil law, you are required to maintain the expected standard, and to drive in a manner that conforms to the standard required for protecting others.

Additional requirements for motor insurance

Any NHS Trust employee must inform their own insurer of any road traffic accident that they are involved in whilst driving during their work activities for the service. Failure to do so may result in your insurance being declared void by your insurers, as you will have failed to disclose your full driving history.

Driving licence checks

Ambulance services have a duty to check driving licences of all staff who drive service vehicles. These checks take place on a regular basis, normally annually (refer to local procedures).

Road traffic collision reporting and incident reporting procedures

Each Service has individual procedures in place for reporting incidents involving motor vehicles. Drivers of service vehicles should ensure full compliance with local procedures.

Emergency driving guidelines

Emergency vehicle drivers are exempt from various requirements of road traffic legislation. The following section offers advice and guidance in relation to the claiming of specific legal exemptions.

Remember!

Whilst attending **any** incident staff **must** consider parking locations carefully, not only for patient/crew access, but more importantly, consider whether it offers the maximum protection to other road users; is there a safer alternative? Your personal safety is paramount, it is vital that the correct use of personal protective clothing (PPE) is adopted, and that maximum visual warning is activated on the responding vehicle.

Legal exemptions

- The statutory speed limit can be exceeded, but only if it is safe to do so. (s.87 Road Traffic Regulation Act (RTRA) 1984 (speed))

- Static, portable and inoperative traffic lights can be treated as a Give Way. (Regulation 36(1)(b) The Traffic Signs Regulations & General Directions 2002 (red light))

- Vehicles may pass on wrong side of keep left/right signs, if progress is likely to be hindered, and no danger is caused to other vehicles, and it can be justified that there were no other alternatives (in exceptional circumstances). (Regulation 15(2) The Traffic Signs Regulations and General Directions 2002)

Road traffic law exemptions

- **Stopping on clearways***
  Road Traffic Regulations Act 1984 s.5

- **Parking within the zig-zag area of a pedestrian crossing***
  Traffic signs regulations and general directions regulation 27(3)(c) 2002
  Remember:
  Increased risk to pedestrians
  Scene safety is paramount
  Ensure police/traffic control assistance

- **Parking within areas controlled by double white/yellow lines***
  Traffic signs regulations and general directions regulation 26(5)(b) 2002
  Remember:
  Consideration of road layout to minimise risks
  Assessment of patient condition and mobility
  Keep parking time to a minimum

* These exemptions may be claimed when dealing with any category of patient, all remaining exemptions may only be claimed whilst engaged on emergencies.

- **Leaving the engine running whilst parked**
  Road vehicles [construction and use] regulations 1986. Regulation 107
  Exemption for non emergency and emergency situations
  Remember:
  Vehicle security/use of 'run lock'
  Heating and lighting factors
  Environmental factors

- **Parking on the offside of the road at night***
  Road vehicles [construction and use] regulations 1986. Regulation 101
  Road vehicle lighting regulations. Regulation 24
  Remember:
  Headlights off
  Leave sidelights on
  Use hazard warning lights
  Use of PPE

- **Parking on a footway/verge/central reservation*** RTRA 1984 s.5
  Bylaws
  Remember:
  Obstruction to pedestrians
  Hazard of soft verges
  Footpath and vehicle damage

- **Exceeding statutory speed limits**
  Road Traffic Regulations Act 1984 (Amended 2006) s.87(1)(2)
  Remember:
  Danger of 'red mist' affecting driver
  Unpredictability of other road users
  Traffic calming measures in place
  Suggested 20mph maximum increase above speed limit
  Increased rate of hazard prioritisation necessary
  Greater density of hazards = reduce speed
  Weather conditions
  Be aware of the limitations of the vehicle and the driver

* These exemptions may be claimed when dealing with any category of
patient, all remaining exemptions may only be claimed whilst engaged on emergencies.

- **Treating a red traffic light as a give way – includes zebra crossing (not traffic controlled)**

  Traffic signs regulations and general directions regulations 33, 34, 35, 36(1)(a), 38(a/b) 2002 Motorway

  Zebra, pelican, equestrian and puffin pedestrian crossing regulations

  Toucan crossings. Regulation 49 2002

  Remember:

  Never attempt to force other road users into illegal manoeuvres

  Always afford precedence to pedestrians showing an intention to use the crossing

  Restrained approach with maximum use of warning equipment

  Are all road users aware of the emergency vehicle?

  Use vehicle positioning on approach to indicate intended route

  Possibility of another emergency vehicle on an opposing route

  Link speed of approach to anticipated light changes to green

  Where no progress can be made, the ambulance should adopt a 'hold back' position and turn audible warnings off, to prevent traffic moving through the red light (this is sometimes referred to as effective non use)

- **Use of audible warnings at night**

  Construction and use regulations. Regulation 99 1986

  Remember:

  Determine the need for an advanced audible warning

  Level of traffic/pedestrian activity

  Consider other audible devices/duration

  Remember siren off = speed off

- **Observing keep left/right signs**

  Traffic signs regulations and general directions 2002 15(2)

  Remember:

  Dangers of returning to the near side

  Essential use of mirrors and signal

  Hazards of central barrier/separate carriageway

  Roundabout entry and direction of travel

  Oncoming traffic

  Pedestrians may only look one way

  Maximum use of audible/visual warnings

  Speed reduction

- **Motorway regulations (where you need to do so in order to avoid or prevent an accident, or to obtain or give the help required at an accident scene)**
  Motorway Traffic (England and Wales) Regulations 1982

  Remember:
  Higher speeds/density of traffic
  Essential use of PPE and visual warnings
  Increased engine/road noise masks sirens
  Use of hard shoulder running
  Parking under police/etc supervision
  Situation if first vehicle on scene

- **Entering a bus lane during its hours of operations**
  Bylaw (possible local operator policy variance for non emergency and use of contra flow bus lanes)

  Remember:
  In emergencies, traffic usually pulls over to the left, foreign vehicles may inadvertently move right
  Parked cars during non operation times
  Check the hours of operation
  Bus lane/street may have shared occupancy
  Proximity of pedestrians
  Avoid contra-flow bus lanes

- **Entering a pedestrian precinct**
  Traffic Signs Regulations and General Directions (TSR&GD) 2002 Bylaw
  Exemption for emergency driving situations

  Remember:
  Speed of entry into precinct
  Speed of negotiation = extreme caution
  Conform to direction of traffic flow
  Consider most suitable audible warning
  Accord pedestrian precedence
  Security of vehicle when parked
  Danger of being blocked in by delivery vehicles, etc

Non exemptions

It is important to remember that drivers of ambulance vehicles cannot claim exemptions for the following:

1. Dangerous driving
2. Dangerous parking
3. Careless driving
4. Failing to stop if involved in a road traffic collision
5. Driving without wearing a seatbelt other than stated in the *Highway Code*
6. Failing to obey a red traffic signal controlling a railway level crossing or fire station
7. Crossing or straddling a solid white line, nearest to you, along the centre of the road when not entitled to do so subject to rule 129 HC

   This means you MUST NOT cross or straddle it unless it is safe and you need to enter adjoining premises or a side road. You may cross the line if necessary, providing the road is clear, to pass a stationary vehicle, or overtake a pedal cycle, horse or road maintenance vehicle, if they are travelling at 10 mph [16km/h] or less.

   Laws RTA 1988 section 36 and TSRGD regulations 10 and 26

8. Failing to obey a one-way traffic sign
9. Failing to obey a no entry sign
10. Failing to obey a stop or give way sign.

Furthermore, these conditions apply even when driving under emergency conditions.

No driver is exempt from driving in a manner that is dangerous, careless or inconsiderate and that may put either lives or property at risk.

Learning outcomes

- Know your responsibilities to drive in a manner that does not constitute 'dangerous', 'careless' or 'inconsiderate' driving.
- Know your obligations under civil law.
- Trust employees procedural requirements regarding motor vehicle insurance.
- Sound knowledge of your Trust's RTC and incident reporting procedures.
- Road traffic law exemptions.
- Road traffic law non exemptions.

Automatic Gearboxes

Correct driving practice is essential in order to get the best from vehicles fitted with automatic transmission and to drive them safely.

Automatic gearboxes and modern derivatives are becoming more common but some drivers are uncertain as how to make the best use of them. These notes, are designed to assist you get the most from your vehicle. A reasonable understanding of the general principles of the automatic gearbox will enable you to make appropriate decisions based on the prevailing circumstances and the performance of your vehicle.

The make-up of the automatic transmission, in the majority of cases, consists of a torque converter and a set of gears. These are fitted to the vehicle in place of a conventional clutch and gearbox.

The torque converter, as the name implies, converts the torque or turning effort of the engine power through the gear ratios to the drive wheels.

Safety

It is vitally important to remember that automatics do not have a clutch pedal. Depressing the footbrake, with the left foot, in the mistaken belief that this is the clutch can have disastrous consequences – particularly if the vehicle is being driven at speed and being followed too closely by another road user.

VDI and pre-driving check
Automatics should always be left in park (P) when not being driven. When carrying out pre-driving check 'selector in P' should be substituted for 'gear lever in neutral'.

Selector options

The selector control can be mounted on the floor, dashboard or steering column (see Figure 2.1). Some vehicles have paddles or push button mechanisms. An illuminated indicator panel (usually mounted on the dashboard) provides visual confirmation of the position currently selected. The basic selector positions are:

- **P-PARK**, should be selected when the vehicle is parked, before the engine is switched off. A check should be made that the selector is in this position before attempting to start the engine. To further ensure safety, the foot brake should be depressed whilst starting the engine. **Never move the lever to the 'P' position whilst the vehicle is in motion**.

- **R-REVERSE**, is usually located next to park in the selector mechanism sequence. The footbrake **must always** be depressed when moving the selector from **P** to **R**, or when moving from **P** through **R** to get to another selector option. The vehicle will begin to move backwards the instant the selector is moved into **R**, **unless the brakes are applied**.

- **N-NEUTRAL**, is selected if it is necessary to tow the vehicle after break down or accident. It should not be selected when making temporary stops in traffic.

- **D-DRIVE**, is the normal operational mode when driving an automatic. As the accelerator is depressed, and the vehicle gathers speed, sensors detect the optimum time to change up to the next highest gear. The change is then made, automatically, without the intervention of the driver. Changes can be detected by watching the rev counter and listening for changes in the engine note. Harsh acceleration can result in jerky changes, whilst smooth and gradual increase in speed may make changes imperceptible to patients and other passengers.

Deceleration, in a vehicle fitted with manual transmission, is relatively straightforward. Releasing pressure on the accelerator pedal slows the engine, and deceleration is achieved by means of engine compression. This is especially effective in lower gears. In the automatic, however, this is not the case. Releasing pressure on the accelerator will not result in a change down to a lower gear, nor is engine compression apparent. This is sometimes referred to as 'run on' and provides a driving sensation similar to 'coasting'. If the vehicle is travelling uphill, then gravity will slow it down. If the vehicle is travelling downhill, the combined effects of run-on and gravity will result in a progressive increase in speed.

For normal driving the lever can remain in 'D' and allow the transmission to make automatic adjustments according to road speed, engine loading and accelerator position.

Figure 2.1 The four positions of the selector lever:

P – Parking Lock: Prevents the vehicle from rolling away when stopped.

R – Reverse: Only engage reverse gear when the vehicle is stationary.

N – Neutral: No power is transmitted from the engine to the drive wheels.

– D+ – Automatic drive using all forward gears and a configuration of 1, 2, 3 and 4 for manual selection, or a symbol such as a plus or minus sign for upward or downward manual changes allowing the vehicle to be driven like a clutchless manual vehicle.

Many drivers of automatics leave the gear selector in D and never consider other options built into the gearbox even though there are times when this might be clearly desirable to optimise flexibility and control of the vehicle. In many cases this is due to ignorance of the potential benefits of using the full range of the gearbox.

Lock down options

These are effective means of controlling the automatic gearbox whilst descending steep gradients or overtaking. The number of lock down options varies, and depends on whether the vehicle being driven has 4, 5 or 6 gears. The number of lock down options will always be less than the total number of gears present, i.e. a five speed gearbox will have four lock down options, whilst a vehicle with four gears will have three lock down choices.

Lock down 1 – This is used on very steep downhill gradients to utilise engine compression to help control speed and lessen the load on the brakes. The vehicle should be brought to a halt at the top of the slope before selecting lock down 1. In lock down 1 the vehicle is locked in first gear and will not change up to any other gear. The selector should be moved back to drive when the descent has been completed.

Lock down 2 – This is used to control speed, on descents, in the same way as lock down 1. As the gear is higher, there is less engine compression and this option is suitable for fairly steep downhill gradients. The selector will not change up to third or any higher gear.

Lock down 3 – This is used for overtaking in a vehicle fitted with 4 gears. It can also be used for controlling speed on moderate downhill gradients in a vehicle fitted with 5 or more gears. Overtaking, in an automatic, can be more hazardous than when driving a vehicle fitted with manual transmission. This is because as speed is increased to complete the manoeuvre, the automatic gearbox is predisposed to change up to the next highest gear. This can result in potentially disastrous loss of power at a critical point in the overtake. Using a lock down option, prior to commencing the overtake, eliminates the possibility and the selector is moved back to drive when the manoeuvre has been completed safely.

Lock down 4/5 – This is used for overtaking, as described above, in vehicles fitted with 5 or 6 gears.

It is essential to remember to move the selector back to drive when the need to utilise lock down has passed. Driving the vehicle for a prolonged period in a lock down option can result in overheating the automatic transmission fluid and causing damage to the transmission system.

Moving the selector is best done when not accelerating. Care must be taken to ensure that the selector is moved the correct number of steps to reach the desired position. Practice is essential to facilitate accuracy when attention cannot be diverted from the road ahead to check the indicator panel.

Creep – if any selector position other than **P** or **N** is selected, and the footbrake or parking brake are not applied, then the vehicle will tend to creep forward or backward at low speed, even when pressure is not applied to the accelerator pedal. The rate of creep will vary in response to the force of gravity. Creep will, consequently, be greater on a downhill slope than an uphill slope. Creep can, and must, be controlled by using the footbrake. It is particularly useful when manoeuvring at low speeds or when negotiating obstacles such as ramps and speed bumps.

Run on – relaxing pressure on the accelerator, whilst driving a vehicle fitted with manual transmission, tends to result in a reduction in speed due to deceleration forces created by engine compression. This is not the case when driving an automatic with the selector set in the **D** position. Indeed, if the vehicle is on a downhill slope, you will notice an increase in speed and will experience a sensation akin to 'coasting' down a hill. Steep downward slopes can produce an alarming sensation of losing control as gravity takes over and vehicle speed rises sharply. The timely and judicious use of lock down (see above) will effectively prevent this potentially dangerous circumstance. When driving on level stretches of road, early relaxation of pressure on the accelerator will facilitate more efficient acceleration sense. Run on is not usually an issue when travelling uphill, as gravity will assist the driver in slowing the speed of the vehicle.

Kick down – this is a useful safety feature that should only be used at times of actual or potential danger. It provides short-term bursts of maximum acceleration, to escape from hazardous circumstances, without the need to move the selector lever. 'Kick' the accelerator' pedal down rapidly and forcefully to the furthest limit of its travel. After a very brief interval, the transmission will change down to the next lowest gear and rapid acceleration will ensue. Holding the pedal down may result in a further subsequent change down and yet more acceleration. You thus have a mechanism to escape from danger by using maximum acceleration when this is appropriate. Relaxing pressure on the accelerator results in loss of acceleration and a change back up to a higher gear. Care must be taken when using kick down. Plan and look well ahead to ensure that the vehicle is not powered out of one dangerous situation and into another.

Summary

Automatics can make driving appear easier by removing the need to make recurring changes of gear whilst concentrating on maintaining smooth clutch control. Diligent application of the above principles will ensure that you get the best from your vehicle whilst maintaining full control without compromising safety margins.

System application using automatic gearboxes

When it is necessary to manually change down and limit the range of gear ratios, the gear lever or change mechanism should be moved to the required position. The owner's manual will describe the most appropriate method. Selecting the ratio is done within the system of car control when the desired speed has been reached and that speed is within the range of the ratio chosen. Most modern systems will override the lever selection and prevent a change to a lower gear if the engine revs or the road speed are too high.

Manually selecting a set of ratios may be in response to a particular hazard where there is a need for more control through use of the accelerator. This will prevent the gear changing up automatically, which may result in the vehicle 'running on' and increasing speed when this is not required. Manually locking a ratio also provides the flexibility to control speed during and after an overtaking manoeuvre, as an alternative to a 'kick-down' or when approaching an area of uncertainty. However, when the specific or general need for flexibility has passed, the '**D**' (Drive) option should be reconsidered.

You should also choose to retain a lower ratio, for instance within a built-up area, in the presence of hazards, to improve control through the accelerator. However, the upper ratio selected should be appropriate to the circumstances. Selecting 3 in a 5 speed automatic box may be suitable for urban driving but 4 may be the better and more flexible choice for winding rural roads. Leaving the gearbox in 'D' may be appropriate for open bends where the flexibility of a lower ratio is not considered necessary.

You should remember that, as with a manual gearbox, selecting a specific ratio on an automatic box should take place when the correct speed for the hazard has been attained. As with a manual gearbox secondary braking should be avoided. Some police forces advocate a more direct manual use of the automatic box, particularly in 'response' situations. However, where a degree of flexibility and maximum performance is neither required nor necessary, the manual override facility must not be used excessively.

When stationary in traffic, even for many minutes, it is not necessary to move the gear lever into neutral because the torque converter absorbs the engine's propulsion force but does not transmit it all to the gearbox. No wear is taking place; in fact, more wear will take place if you engage neutral then engage a drive gear when it is possible to move off. Most gearboxes will automatically select first gear when the vehicle becomes stationary.

While guidance may be given regarding the correct actions in certain circumstances, not all eventualities can be covered. The following is intended as general guidance in some common sets of circumstances.

- **Stopping:** You should apply the footbrake when moving the gear lever when the vehicle is stationary. Set the parking brake, (for temporary stops longer than 10 seconds) as many vehicles will 'creep' and some vehicles may have a tendency to lurch. For stops in traffic, at junctions and at traffic lights leave the selector in **D**. There is no need to move into neutral, as no damage will result.

- **At roundabouts:** Engage the appropriate gear in manual mode on the approach to the hazard.

- **On bends:** Non severe single bends can normally be negotiated in **D**. For a series of bends manually select a gear with a suitable ratio prior to the first bend, and on exit from that bend, when the accelerator is eased to set the vehicle up for the next bend, the vehicle will not automatically change up and the driver will have the benefit of engine braking which will give better control.

- **Overtaking:** Depending on the circumstances, use either a planned, predetermined lower ratio lock or the 'kick-down'. If acceleration is needed followed by deceleration to fit into a gap, manually select a lower gear or 'locking' the ratio before the start of the manoeuvre may be beneficial.

- **Steep hills:** When descending steep hills in **D**, the vehicle will tend to drop into its highest ratio. This will result in excessive use of the brakes. Although brakes on automatics are larger than on their manual counterparts, 'brake fade' can still create a problem but manually locking a low ratio provides compression braking to enhance flexibility and braking control. Conversely, when ascending a steep hill, manually locking a ratio may also provide better control and improve smoothness if the vehicle is hunting between two ratios.

- Never select **P** while the vehicle is in motion, as it will cause major damage or an accident by locking the transmission.

- Only engage reverse gear when the vehicle is stationary, otherwise the transmission could be damaged.

- Always ensure that the footbrake is on before engaging either '**D**' or '**R**' from stationary.

- DO NOT engage '**D**' or '**R**' with a high revving engine.

- Check that you do not knock the gear lever accidentally as this could change the gear out of '**D**' drive to 4th.

General

In unusual circumstances when the gearbox is continually changing up and down between two gears, manually selecting an appropriate ratio may prevent undue wear of the gearbox components.

It is not necessary to either kick-down or change down manually for a hazard simply because you would change down if driving a car with a manual gearbox when negotiating that same hazard. The modern automatic gearbox is designed to select the correct ratio for the speed and throttle setting, and it does so very well. A manual intervention should be a considered option and planned to give a specific advantage or benefit according to the circumstances encountered.

As with all aspects of driving, this technique is not carved in tablets of stone. There may well be other occasions when you judge it necessary to manually override the gearbox and, if that is the case, then do it. But do not make excessive use of the manual holds and return to 'D' when the need has passed.

3

Vehicle Operating Systems

The key fob

Figure 3.1 illustrates a standard ambulance key fob.

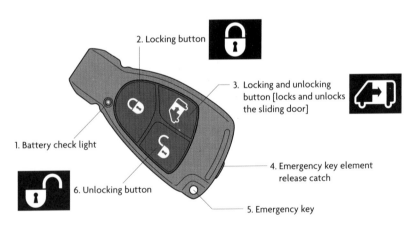

Figure 3.1 Key fob.

At the top edge of the fob is a slide button, when moved it releases the key within the fob, this key opens the driver door should the fob fail to operate due to battery malfunction or damage.

Care should be given not to leave the key fob in the vehicle; the vehicle may automatically lock after 90 seconds if all the doors are closed.

Braking

The standard dashboard warning signals are shown in Figure 3.2.

Brake assist system (BAS)

The brake assist system operates in emergency braking situations. If the brake pedal is depressed quickly BAS automatically increases the brake pressure, thereby reducing the stopping distance.

If BAS malfunctions the vehicle will still have its full brake boosting effect however the stopping distance may increase.

Antilock brake system (ABS)

When ABS is activated you will be able to steer and brake without the wheels locking; you will feel a pulsating of the brake pedal.

Electronic brake-power distribution (EBV)

Electronic brake-power distribution monitors and controls the brake pressure on rear wheels in order to improve handling during braking.

  ESP malfunction

  ASR or BAS malfunction

  Brake fluid level low or EBV malfunction

  ABS malfunction

  Brake pads/linings worn

Figure 3.2 Dashboard warning signals.

Telma Retarders

The Telma Retarder is a low maintenance, friction-free system that provides exceptional performance at all road speeds slowing the vehicle yet always ensuring a smooth ride for patient and crew. The fully automatic control system is activated by the action of the driver depressing the brake pedal, and requires no additional driver operations and no special training other than an 'awareness' of the system.

The standstill system automatically detects when the vehicle is moving, enabling the retarder system.

The Telma Retarder system reaction time is virtually instantaneous. This makes for optimum compatibility with the Antilock Braking System (ABS). Application of the foot brake operates the circuits in the control box, which close, and energises the retarder, which applies the 'friction free' braking torque to the rear wheels, slowing the vehicle down, the red 'R' switch will illuminate during this function (see Figure 3.3).

Figure 3.3 The red R switch.

The Telma Retarder system has shown to absorb over 80% of braking applications automatically. This helps keep brake temperatures low. High brake temperatures mean high brake wear, high maintenance costs, more vehicle downtime and the use of other brake associated parts.

Substantial savings are possible over the life of the vehicles in parts (brake pads and discs) and maintenance labour. A major saving is shown to be achievable over a typical 5-year life of the vehicle, not including additional savings on items of expenditure such as callipers, hubs, seals and bearings that might also have to be replaced.

In braking, large amounts of energy from the vehicle's momentum are converted into heat in the braking system. Heavy braking at high speeds can create huge increases in temperature, giving rise to all the well-known problems – brake-fade, excessive lining wear, damage to discs, pads, etc.

The Telma Retarder system, although very smooth in its performance, is a powerful additional braking system and will virtually eliminate all chances of brake fade by maintaining friction materials at a safe operating temperature.

The Telma Retarder system can help reduce overall stopping distances, providing that tyre adhesion is maintained, giving obvious benefits to the crew, the medical staff, patients and other road users. In tests carried out, under relatively heavy service braking levels of 50%, at a speed of just 30 mph (49 kph), the Telma Retarder can reduce the total stopping distance by 3 metres (10 feet).

The Telma system slows the vehicle via the rear axle, and, under braking, contributes to keeping the vehicle level eliminating most of the front-end 'dipping'. This provides a considerable improvement in vehicle stability under braking, both in a straight line and on cornering, with reduced 'roll' of the vehicle and a greater sense of confidence in the overall handling.

The Retarder system is a very reliable, robust, self-sealed system that generally requires very little in the way of maintenance other than a periodic inspection.

Acceleration skid control (ASR)

This improves traction, that is, the transfer of power from the tyres to the road surface, for a sustained period; thus it also improves the driving stability of the vehicle. ASR assists you when pulling away and accelerating, especially on smooth and slippery surfaces. ASR brakes individual drive wheels and limits the engine torque to prevent the drive wheels from spinning. When ASR intervenes, the warning light in the instrument cluster flashes. DO NOT deactivate ASR.

Electronic stability program (ESP)

This monitors driving stability and detects a tendency of the vehicle to under/over steer (skidding) in good time. It stabilises the vehicle by braking individual wheels as well as limiting the engine power output; it greatly assists you when driving on wet or slippery road surfaces. The warning light in the instrument cluster panel lights up when ESP is intervening. ESP cannot reduce the risk of an accident if you drive too fast. ESP is unable to override the laws of physics.

PSM module

This relates to electrical functions, which convert data input to operate the electrics on the vehicle and is a workshop function.

Emergency lighting control system

Cancel and pre check

This is a special feature button that can only be activated when the ignition and handbrake are both on.

When pressed and held for 5 seconds it activates every function that can be visually inspected, individually and sequentially in a pre determined order.

Arrive scene mode

If the ignition is on, the ignition security feature is the first function to be activated, allowing you to remove the ignition key and leave the engine running securely, depending on the specification the engine rpm may increase from idle.

If the handbrake is released the engine will stall.

Siren activation

The siren is activated and the sound/tone changed by pressing the pedal where the clutch should be or by pressing the horn at the centre of the steering wheel dependant on vehicle type.

Risk of accidents

To reduce the risk of accidents, remember:

- This vehicle will not pass through 6'-6" pinch points or indicated width of vehicle.

- If any of the icons below light up whilst on a journey, there may be a malfunction in the electronic brake-power distribution (EBV). You should therefore drive with particular care.

- If ASR is deactivated there is an increased risk that the brake system of the vehicle could overheat and could be damaged.

- If the warning light in the instrument cluster flashes proceed as follows:
  - do not deactivate ASR under any circumstances.
  - only depress the accelerator pedal as far as necessary when pulling away.
  - adapt your driving style to suit the prevailing road and weather conditions, otherwise the vehicle could start to skid

- There is a malfunction if the ESP indicator icon is constantly lit when the engine is running. If ESP malfunctions, engine power output maybe reduced.

Learning outcomes

- Carry out a comprehensive vehicle daily inspection (VDI) and pre-driving check (PDC).

- Competently operate all selector options: park, reverse, neutral, drive.

- Demonstrate the lock down options.

- Recognise the differences between manual and automatic transmissions in regards to 'creep', 'run on', and 'kick down'.

Principles of Cornering

In order to safely negotiate a bend, the principles below must be followed:

- correct positioning of the vehicle on the approach side
- correct speed for the corner or bend
- correct gear for the speed
- ability to stop safely within the distance you can see to be clear.

Safety factors

If these principles are adhered to the following safety factors will be apparent as the vehicle is about to leave the corner or bend:

- it will be on the correct side of the road
- it will remain there
- it will be capable of being stopped in the distance that you can see to be clear
- applying the principles of corners and bends in conjunction with road signs and markings increases patient comfort, vehicle sympathy, stability and view which also increases a safety.

For many years now the commentary for principles of cornering has been accepted as:

- correct position of the vehicle on the approach side which will be nearside for a right-hand bend, and just left of centre line for a left-hand bend, this should be adopted at the latest opposite the road sign or in the presence of deflection arrows, no later than the second arrow or in any case, in time to allow the rest of the system stages to be concluded before the bend.

- right choice of speed. This is selected by reading the limit point and considerations of:
  - what can be seen?
  - what cannot be seen?
  - what could reasonably be expected to happen
  - what to do if things turn out differently (the contingency plan)
  - adjusting speed by acceleration or by braking as necessary
  - all of the above being done before the first deflection arrow.
- the correct gear for the speed is selected before the second arrow (if present) or in any case before steering commences. If overlapping is evident, then too much speed is being carried into the bend and control is greatly reduced.
- the vehicle should maintain constant speed whilst negotiating the bend. Reading the limit point and fine adjustments made with acceleration sense is essential to reduce dangerous cornering forces.

Learning outcomes

- The four principles of cornering.
- Safety factors in relation to cornering.
- What will determine the correct choice of speed.

5

Speed and Safety

Speed limits

Whilst exempt from adhering to speed limits, there still remains a statutory requirement to maintain safety and to offer the maximum protection to other road users – legal exemptions do not include driving at speed in a manner which is dangerous, nor driving without due care and attention. Driving above the limit is only acceptable when it is safe to do so.

Road, traffic and weather conditions should be taken into consideration when deciding on an appropriate speed to make progress.

It is recommended that whilst responding under blue light conditions, vehicles should not exceed 20mph above the speed limit.

(See Appendix 5 for further information on speed and safety/feet per second.)

Learning outcomes

- The statutory requirement to offer maximum protection to other road users.
- The recommended speed limit during emergency response driving.

Audible and Visual Warnings

Emergency warning equipment (EWE)

Blue flashing lights and sirens influence the behaviour of other road users due to the presence of the emergency vehicle and the urgency of the journey being undertaken. They do not give any legal entitlement to claim precedence. You should also be at all times conscious that if you have EWE fitted to a vehicle the public has a right to receive the warning the equipment is designed to give.

This can cause problems for emergency drivers when other road users slow to let them pass where road markings indicate no overtaking.

Appearance and markings

Emergency ambulance vehicles, due to the nature of the work, are exposed to hazardous activities on a regular basis, the urgency of their function provides for certain exemptions to driving law. However, you and the trust are obliged, under the corporate manslaughter act and road traffic bill, to afford, at all times, the maximum protection to other road users. The presence of an emergency vehicle often influences the behaviour of other road users and pedestrians, and for these reasons, emergency ambulances are fitted with visual and/or audible warnings to alert road users.

Visual warnings on an ambulance can be of two types – either **passive** or **active**.

Passive visual warnings

Passive visual warnings are usually part of the design of the vehicle, and involve the use of high contrast patterns. Older ambulances are more likely to have their pattern painted on, whereas modern ambulances generally carry retro-reflective designs which reflect light from car headlights or torches. Popular patterns include 'checker board' (alternate coloured squares, sometimes called 'Battenberg', named after the type of cake), chevrons (arrowheads – often pointed towards the front of the vehicle if on the side, or pointed vertically upwards on the rear) or stripes along the side (these were the first type of retro-reflective device introduced, as the original reflective material, invented by 3M, only came in tape form). In addition to retro-reflective markings, some services now have the vehicles painted in a bright (sometimes fluorescent) yellow or orange for maximum visual impact. In Europe this colour is defined as Euro Yellow RAL 1016 for emergency service vehicles.

Another passive marking form is the word ambulance spelled out in reverse on the front of the vehicle. This enables drivers of other vehicles to more easily identify an approaching ambulance in their rear view mirrors.

Active visual warnings

The active visual warnings are usually in the form on flashing coloured lights (sometimes known as 'beacons' or 'light bars'). These flash in order to attract the attention of other road users as the ambulance approaches, or to provide warning to motorists approaching a stopped ambulance in a dangerous position on the road. Common colours for ambulance warning beacons are blue and rear facing alternating red lights.

In order to increase safety, it is a legal requirement to have 360° coverage with active warnings, improving the chance of the vehicle being seen from all sides.

Audible warnings

In addition to visual warnings, ambulances are fitted with audible warnings, sometimes known as sirens, which can alert people to the presence of an ambulance before they can be seen. The first audible warnings were mechanical bells, mounted to either the front or roof of the ambulance. Most modern ambulances are now fitted with electronic sirens, which can produce a range of different noises. Ambulance services may specifically train their drivers to use different siren tones in different situations. For instance, on a clear road, approaching a junction, the 'wail' setting may be used, which gives a long up and down variation, with an unbroken tone, whereas, in heavy slow traffic a 'yelp' setting may be preferred, which is like a wail but speeded up, and is not as subject to sound deflection causing confusion as the direction of approach of the emergency vehicle.

Modern siren technology also includes 'dual tone' sirens, which can emit two different siren tones simultaneously and is beneficial for manoeuvring through heavy traffic or approaching intersections.

The speakers for modern sirens can be integral to the light bar, hidden in or flush to the grill. Ambulances can additionally be fitted with an air horn and audible warnings.

A more recent development is the use of the RDS system of car radios, whereby the ambulance can be fitted with a short range FM transmitter, set to RDS code 31, which interrupts the radio of all cars within range, in the manner of a traffic broadcast, but in such a way that the user of the receiving radio is unable to opt out of the message (as with traffic broadcasts). This feature is built into every RDS radio for use in national emergency broadcast systems, but short range units on emergency vehicles can prove an effective means of alerting traffic to their presence. It is, however, unlikely that this system could replace audible warnings, as it is unable to alert pedestrians, or those not using a compatible radio.

General points

- You must be fully aware that attitudes related to driving under blue light conditions are influenced considerably by any intrusive thoughts, however insignificant as they may seem, (i.e. focusing on the potential incident that is being responded to, personal influences relating to work or private life) all of which shut down the decision making process. A driving response protocol needs to be retained which provides the operator with the ability to perform regardless of outside influences.

- You must bear in mind that you may be liable to prosecution if your actions are such that you fall below a safe standard.

- The Ambulance Service can claim exemption only if the vehicle was engaged on an emergency call. If a service employee is captured on a surveillance camera you may be liable to prosecution unless you can demonstrate you were active on an emergency call and at the time of camera activation the vehicle was being utilised for ambulance purposes.

- In the event of a solo response driver (SRD) remaining with the patient en-route to the hospital, (due to their advanced clinical skills), one of the ambulance crew members may be asked to drive the solo response vehicle (SRV) to the receiving hospital. When this situation arises, the SRV must not utilise emergency warning equipment and will adhere to all road traffic regulations.

Learning outcomes

- The use of emergency warning equipment [EWE].
- Passive and active visual warnings.
- Use of audible warnings.

7

Lighting Regulations

The following information is a simplification of:

- The Road Vehicles Lighting Regulations 1989 (1 November 1989)
- The Road Vehicles Lighting (Amendment) Regulations 2005 (21 October 2005)
- The Road Vehicles Lighting (Amendment) (No.2) Regulations 2005 (12 December 2005)

Changes made in 2005

A number of small changes were made to the lighting regulations in 2005. These are shown below where appropriate, but are summarised as:

- emergency vehicles no longer have to have a motor (e.g. cycles)
- anyone can use flashing lights on their cycles (1–4 flashes per second, equal amount of time on and off, usual colours)
- cycles with lights in the pedals or attached to the wheels are now permitted
- revenue and customs are allowed to use blue flashing lights when investigating a serious crime
- an abnormal load escort vehicle is defined and allowed to use amber flashing lights above 25mph
- officially authorised vehicle examiners can drive a vehicle on the road that does not have the correct lighting if it is going to, or returning from, a test, and they don't believe the defects are dangerous.

Only emergency vehicles can be fitted with a blue flashing light, or anything that looks like a blue flashing light, whether it is in working order or not.

All your lights need to be clean and working. Reflectors just need to work. The exceptions to this are when:

- the light does not need to be seen because you are towing a trailer which has lights
- a light has just stopped working on your current journey
- you have tried everything reasonable to fix it.

The only times when you can use your blue flashing lights are when you are:

- at the scene of an emergency
- responding to an emergency
- wanting to let people know you are there
- wanting to let people know that there is a hazard on the road.

Further details

The information in this section is provided in good faith to give an overview of current legislation. Parts remain crown copyright. DTAG cannot be held responsible for any mistakes or misinterpretations that exist. The full legislation on lighting is available to view on the website of the Office of Public Sector Information (formerly HM Stationary Office). Below are the links to the relevant parts of the road vehicle lighting regulation:

Index – part I – Part II – Part III – Part IV _ Amendment – Amendment No. 2

Learning outcomes

- The changes made to lighting regulations 2005.

8

Reversing and Manoeuvring

Introduction

A significant percentage of collisions involving ambulance service NHS Trust vehicles occur whilst carrying out low speed manoeuvres, especially those involving reversing. More collisions occur whilst reversing than in any other category. Many, if not all of these incidents can be avoided if basic standard procedures are diligently and consequently put into practice, and often negligence has a major influence. This will reduce not only repair costs but also vehicle down time, whilst promoting safety and reducing risk of personal injury.

Good theory and practice

The Highway Code sets out general rules and advice on reversing and manoeuvring for the benefit of all drivers. In addition, the following advice is given:

- Only turn the steering wheel whilst the vehicle is moving, thereby avoiding damage to the tyres, steering linkage and any power assisted steering mechanisms.

- Utilise slow vehicle speed in conjunction with rapid hand movements, on the steering wheel, when manoeuvring in confined areas.

- Turn the steering in the direction of the next vehicle movement just before ending the previous movement.

- Keep the vehicle moving slowly, controlling speed by engaging/disengaging clutch or in the case of automatic transmission using the footbrake to control the speed.

- Carefully observe the front of the vehicle, as it swings left or right, whilst carrying out reversing turns.

- Consider using hazard warning lights to illuminate the area, if reversing lights fail in conditions of reduced visibility.

- Avoid over revving the engine, remembering that engine tick over may be sufficient on level ground.

The importance of team work

Very few, if any, reversing collisions occur when correct standard procedure is being followed, i.e. when the attendant is assisting the driver from the correct vantage point outside the vehicle. This vantage point should always be at the rear nearside (unless there are unusual circumstances which make this unsafe or impractical).

With the driver in the driving seat and the attendant at the rear nearside responsibilities are shared as follows:

The driver is responsible for:

- making sure that the attendant can be clearly seen in the nearside mirror before commencing the manoeuvre

- controlling the speed of the vehicle

- bringing the vehicle to an immediate halt if the attendant disappears from view

- ensuring safety at the front and offside of the vehicle.

The attendant is responsible for:

- taking up a position at the rear nearside of the vehicle, in a position where they can be seen in the driver's nearside mirror

- ensuring that their signals remain visible, in the driver's nearside mirror, by adjusting their position as the vehicle moves

- ensuring safety at the rear and nearside of the vehicle.

The driver and attendant should discuss and agree an appropriate plan before commencing the manoeuvre. Hand and arm signals (Figure 8.1) can be augmented by verbal signs. Opening the nearside window will facilitate this. If the major hazard is to the rear of the nearside, the driver should concentrate on following the attendant's signals, with occasional glances to the front of the vehicle and offside mirror to ensure safety. If the major hazard is to the front or offside, the driver should concentrate on these areas, with occasional glances in the nearside mirror to ensure safety.

The attendant must not stand in a position directly between a moving vehicle and a stationary object (e.g. a wall or other vehicle). Where it is impossible or impractical for the attendant to take up a position at the rear nearside, then the best alternative should be adopted. Extra care should be taken in these circumstances.

Extra care should also be taken if an attendant is not present or available. Consideration should be given to obtaining assistance if a suitable person is available. The driver has full responsibility for the safety of the manoeuvre in these circumstances.

Hands should move vertically. Moving horizontally may mean one or both hands are out of the mirror's range of view.

It is essential that the driver does not rely on the technology of audible reverse sensors if fitted to the vehicle!

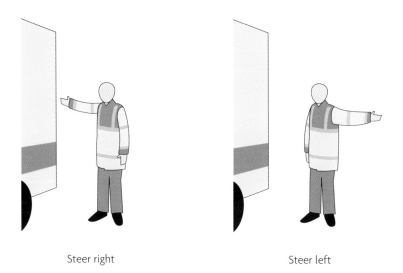

Steer right   Steer left

Straight back

Stop   Clearance

Figure 8.1 An attendant using arm and hand signals.

Learning outcomes

- Good theory and practice for operating a vehicle during a reverse manoeuvre.
- Driver responsibilities.
- Attendant responsibilities.
- Demonstrate competence in practical application.

Attending
Motorway Incidents

Aim

To provide a uniform and consistent approach to incidents occurring on motorways and dual carriageways by ambulance personnel, and members of the other emergency services.

These procedures have been written with reference to Practice Advice on the Policing of Roads (National Centre for Policing Excellence 2007).

You are reminded that the scene of any SERIOUS or FATAL road traffic collision is considered a CRIME scene by the police and although it should not interfere with the care and treatment of patients which is paramount, you are asked to be mindful on scene and minimise unnecessary disturbance of potential evidence if possible.

> Ambulance staff attending any incident on a motorway or dual carriageway will wear personal protective equipment (PPE): high visibility jacket (fastened at the front) and hard helmet will be worn at every incident, no matter how minor it may appear. Serious head injuries have been sustained by members of the emergency services who have not worn any head protection and have been struck by objects and stones thrown up by vehicles passing at high speeds.

These are the **minimum** protection measures staff must take. Any further protection required **must** be decided by staff following their risk assessment of the incident.

Approach

Motorways and dual carriageways present ambulance staff with unique problems due to the high volume of vehicles and the speeds at which they travel. A relatively minor incident can rapidly expand to involve a large number of vehicles. Any incident may lead to a large build up of traffic causing difficulties for attending vehicles.

Different methods of approach to incidents have been devised dependant on differing traffic conditions.

Whenever possible, ambulances should approach using the main carriageway, usually lane two or three (see Figure 9.1). This allows other traffic to react in a normal manner, when hearing or seeing an approaching ambulance to moving to the left. Do not use lane one as this may cause drivers to move left onto the hard shoulder where other vehicles may be parked.

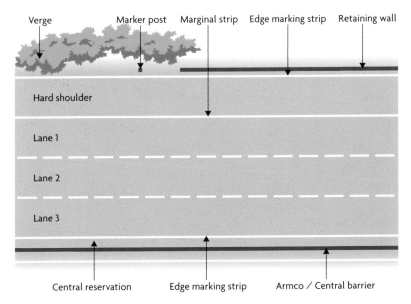

Figure 9.1 Layout of a motorway.

Completely blocked: slow moving or stationary traffic

If the motorway or dual carriageway is completely blocked by slow moving or stationary traffic, then the approach may require the use of the hard shoulder. The following should apply when using the hard shoulder.

1. Traffic on the main carriageway is **moving slowly**: Approach using the hard shoulder with visual warning equipment activated (blue lights and flashing headlights) only. **Do not use sirens**. The use of sirens has on occasions caused drivers to move left onto the hard shoulder into the path of emergency vehicles. The normal road horn can be used to indicate your presence if required.

2. When traffic on the main carriageway is **stationary**: Approach along the hard shoulder with all emergency warning equipment [EWE] activated, visual aids and sirens. Members of the public may sometimes get out of their vehicles to stretch their legs or to see what is going on and may walk onto the hard shoulder.

The use of the hard shoulder requires drivers to exercise extreme caution. The road surface may have loose grit and gravel, oil and other objects present, which would normally be cleared from the carriageway by passing traffic. Vehicles may be parked, without lights at night if broken down. People may be walking on the hard shoulder to or from the emergency telephones. Speeds must be restrained with due regard for the circumstances.

Blockage or closure

When an incident leads to the blockage or closure of the motorway, the police may direct drivers to turn round and drive back to the preceding exit. If this is taking place you will be informed by the police at the junction where the traffic is being directed off the motorway. In this circumstance then the normal rules of the road apply.

- Drive on the left in lane one, not the hard shoulder
- Use visual aids (blue lights and flashing headlights)
- Keep your speed down.

Traffic, which has been turned around, will be kept to their left, in single file at a slow speed by the police.

When the motorway or dual carriageway is blocked or closed you may be directed to approach or leave an incident in the wrong direction by the police. The same procedure applies:

- drive on the left

- use visual aids (blue lights and flashing headlights)

- keep your speed down

- remember other emergency vehicles may be travelling towards you on the same carriageway.

Follow the directions of police officers at all times. Some of the traffic control may be directed by Highways Agency support staff.

Parking

When arriving on scene the crews must perform their own risk assessment, taking into account the directions of other ambulance staff or agencies already present to ensure their own safety.

Parking at a scene already protected by the police or other agency

If the scene is already protected by police or vehicles from other agencies, i.e. Fire brigade or Highways Agency, then ambulances should ideally park at the front of the incident, within the coned off area (Figure 9.2, page 40).

Once parked within the safe area blue lights and flashing headlights should be turned off. Evidence has shown that the risks from 'rubber necking' motorists is significantly reduced as the number of blue flashing lights visible is reduced.

Police vehicles parked at the rear of the scene will provide rear facing blue and red lights.

Parking at unprotected scene, first emergency vehicle on scene

If you are the first emergency vehicle to arrive at a scene, your own safety is paramount. A full risk assessment must be undertaken.

Incidents on the hard shoulder

- If the incident is confined to the hard shoulder, stop your vehicle 50m before the incident in a **straight** line with the carriageway. Turn the front wheel towards the nearside if there is no physical barrier or obstruction.

- If you are parked next to a barrier or other obstruction, i.e. bridge support, turn the front wheels outward toward the carriageway.

- If the vehicle is then struck from behind it will be steered away from you and not pushed straight towards the incident.

- Switch off **forward** facing blue lights and flashing headlights where possible. Use rear facing blue and/or red lights if fitted, side lights and hazard lights. Keep the rear doors **closed** as much as possible to utilise the reflective, high visibility markings.

NB. Dependent on some local police authorities, some forces advocate that emergency vehicles attending motorway incidents leave ALL their visual warning activated, candidates on driver training should be guided by their trust's policy.

When walking stay behind the barrier if possible, if no barrier then stay as far away from the live carriageway as you can. When possible watch the approaching traffic.

Incidents in lanes 1, 2, 3 or combination

If you are first on scene of an incident on any of the carriageways, the vehicle may be placed in a **fend off** position. This involves using the vehicle to block one or more lanes (refer to local trust procedures). **This is extremely hazardous and should be performed with upmost caution.**

- A vehicle used for fend off must be 50m back from the incident, using all rear facing visual devices: blue lights, rear flashing red lights, side lights, fog lights and hazard lights.

- The vehicle should be positioned to afford maximum use of rear visual devices and reflective/hi-visibility markings.

- If parking to fend off lane one, the vehicle should park at a slight angle, but not intrude into lane two.

- If it is necessary to fend off lane two, the vehicle should park at an angle to obstruct lane one and two. Do not intrude into lane three.

- If it is necessary to fend off lane three, adopt the same principle as for lane one. Do not intrude into lane two.

- If it is necessary to fend off lanes two and three, adopt the same principle as for lanes one and two.

The police will allow ambulance staff to block as many lanes as necessary for their own and patient's safety.

- When parking in a fend off position ensure the front wheels are turned in a safe direction to reduce the risk of the vehicle being pushed into the incident if it is collided with.

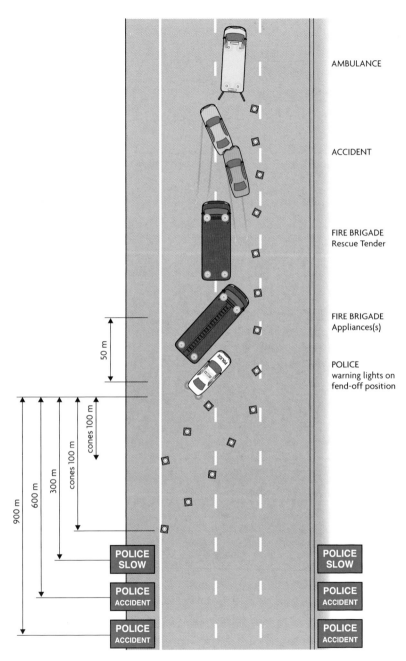

Figure 9.2 Parking in coned off area.

For High Dependency Service (HDS), Patient Transport Service (PTS), service officers' cars and Basics doctors see Appendix 1.

Once parked in a fend off position, no one should return to the vehicle unless absolutely necessary.

Keep your eye on the passing traffic; never assume it is safe. Research has shown that a percentage of drivers cannot distinguish a stationary vehicle on a motorway from one which is moving.

Situation reports (SITREPS)

If you are the first emergency vehicle on scene you should provide control with the following information as soon as possible:

- the nearest marker post number (Figure 9.3). This will confirm your location to within one tenth of a km
- the number and types of vehicles involved
- any hazardous loads
- which lanes of the motorway are involved
- direction of travel, e.g. north.

Figure 9.3 Example of a marker post. The figures are a distance in kilometres from a set point and will give your location within 100 metres. Thus, this post is 25.3km from the defined point.

This information will be relayed to the police motorway control, who will activate the matrix signs if available, to assist in your protection and warn approaching motorists.

Always use the terms 'lane one, two or three', **not** slow, middle or fast. Subsequent sitreps should follow with normal information and requests for further vehicles etc, and should include:

- number of casualties
- types of injuries
- number of vehicles required
- helicopter required (see Appendix 2)
- assistance from other agencies, i.e. fire and rescue
- notifying hospitals, etc.

Keep control regularly informed.

Leaving scene

Leaving the scene and rejoining the moving traffic is extremely hazardous. Drivers passing the scene may be too busy 'rubber necking' to notice you moving.

If you have a clear path in front of you, proceed in a straight line in that lane or hard shoulder until you have built up your speed to match the traffic around you before changing lanes. Keep your rear blue lights on until you have rejoined the normal traffic flow, then turn them off if not conveying the patient as an emergency.

If your path away from the scene is obstructed do not attempt to pull into a live lane of traffic without the assistance of a police officer. Build your speed quickly to match the traffic around you and then turn off your blue lights, etc., unless required for the journey.

Learning outcomes

- The importance of personal protective equipment (PPE).
- How to approach motorway incidents when:
  - traffic is moving slowly
  - traffic is stationary.
- Use of the hard shoulder.
- How to approach
  - when the motorway is blocked
  - using the wrong direction.
- Parking on the motorway (protected).
- Parking on the motorway (unprotected).
- Incidents on the hard shoulder.
- Incidents in lanes 1, 2 and 3.
- HDS, PTS attending motorway incidents.
- Situation reports (SITREPS).
- Leaving the scene.

Escorting Vehicles

Normally this would be done using police motorcycles. One positioned at the front of the ambulance whose role it is to maintain a safe and constant speed. Another is positioned on the offside of the ambulance visible in the offside wing mirror. The final motorcycle is positioned to block off traffic at the next major hazard such as a junction, or a roundabout.

As the ambulance goes through the hazard, the bike controlling the hazard takes up a position on the offside of the ambulance. The bike that was in this position has already moved up to control the next hazard.

It is imperative that the ambulance speed does not exceed 35–40 MPH for the safety of the motorcycles, and the comfort and safety of the patient and healthcare professional working in the back of the vehicle.

The above procedure has been offered by members of the Police Driver Standards Group. Other procedures are in operation around the country and it is in the interests of all services to work across boundaries and work within written local policies and procedures.

- There is currently **no provision or exemption** for ambulance solo response drivers to perform escorts for ambulances, regardless of the circumstances.
- Vehicles travelling under emergency conditions, with visual and audible warnings, should not travel in convoy. Other road users may be unable to clearly identify the number of vehicles approaching and may not expect more

than one emergency vehicle. If the situation requires a number of vehicles to travel to the same incident, then consideration should be given to an appropriate distance being maintained between these vehicles.

Learning outcomes

- Police escorts.
- The non provision of solo responders providing escorts.

Appendices

Appendix 1: HDS, PTS, Officers' Cars and BASICS Doctors

HDS vehicles must only be sent to motorway incidents if a confirmed safe coned area has been set up. They should then follow the same parking arrangements as Emergency and Utility (E&U) vehicles within this coned area. HDS vehicles must not be used to fend off if these vehicles have inadequate blue lights or adequate markings, no daytime high visibility and minimal night time reflective markings to be safely seen by traffic travelling at speed. (Refer to local trust policy.)

PTS vehicles must only attend incidents where the motorway has been closed or a confirmed safe coned area has been set up. They should then follow the same parking arrangements as E&U vehicles. PTS vehicles must never be used to fend off if they have no emergency lights or suitable markings.

Officers' cars and Basics doctors attending must not be used to fend off. Although they have blue lights, often many are dark in colour and have no hi-visibility markings. They should park in the coned area, toward the front ensuring they do not hinder the exit of vehicles.

If any of these vehicles come across or arrive first at the scene of an incident they should:

- park in front of the incident and switch on any visual warnings available
- inform control of the information required in the first 'sitrep'
- perform an individual risk assessment and if unsafe remain in their vehicle and not approach the incident until suitable scene protection is present.

   This can be very difficult but staff must not be tempted to put themselves in danger except in the immediate saving of life.

HDS and PTS staff must not attend unless they have the correct PPE suitable to attend incidents on motorways or dual carriageways.

Appendix 2: Air Ambulance

If you request the attendance of the air ambulance (Air Amb), you must inform the police officers on scene at the earliest opportunity. Control will inform motorway police control that the Air Amb is attending.

Extra officers may be required, as the attendance of the Air Amb will require the closure of the motorway or dual carriageway in both directions if it is intending to land on the road. If you are informed by control that they have mobilised the Air Amb, inform the police officers at the scene as soon as possible for the same reasons.

Appendix 3: Highways Agency Traffic Officers

Where there is no injury or alleged offence, the Highways Agency Traffic Officers (HATOs) service will lead in the management of incidents to:

- manage congestion
- ensure rapid and safe removal of obstructions
- assist vulnerable road users.

The police will maintain scene control for incidents involving:

Figure A3.1 HATO vehicle.

- injury or death
- criminality
- threats to public order and safety
- allegations of criminality or threats to public order and safety
- significant coordination of emergency responders.

Powers for HATOs are detailed in the Traffic Management Act 2004. Section 4 of the Act clarifies the legal relationship between police and HATOs, and states that:

(1) *A traffic officer (HATO) shall, when carrying out his duties, comply with any direction of a police constable.*

(2) *Subject to that, a traffic officer (HATO) designated by an authorised person shall, when carrying out his duties, comply with any direction of the appropriate national authority.*

Ambulance staff must note that HATOs have restricted powers. They are trained to deal with, and may only be used for, the following purposes on the strategic road network:

- maintaining or improving the movement of traffic
- preventing or reducing congestion
- avoiding danger to persons or traffic, or the risk of any such danger arising
- preventing damage to anything on or near the road.

The main powers granted to HATOs are:

- power to stop or direct traffic including cyclists and rolling road blocks
- power to direct vehicles for traffic surveys
- power to direct persons on foot
- power to place temporary traffic signs.

Appendix 4: Driving Commentary Examples

The reasons for giving a commentary whilst driving are:

1. To help students cultivate distant and/or detailed observations
2. To develop logical reasoning and planning
3. To assist the Instructor to 'assess' the student's degree of observations and line of reasoning.

Introduction
1. Type of area
2. Speed limit
3. Weather conditions
4. Traffic volume.

Examples

> *I'm driving on a single carriageway road with one lane in each direction. The road is divided by central lane markings and the surface is dry and is conducive to firm braking. It's a residential area with a speed limit of 30 mph ...*

The object is to form a 'word picture' of the changing scene around the vehicle. Features described should include:
1. Identifying the hazard
2. Action to be taken
3. Reasons for that action.

Points regarding system application should be included where appropriate and when convenient. It is most important that all comments in relation to identifying hazards and the action contemplated are concluded (see Table A4.1).

Table A4.1 Commentary examples for specific hazards.

Feature	Reasoning and driving actions
Garage forecourt on nearside	Clear, no danger or vehicles present, I am slowing down and/or moving out, increasing the margin of safety.
Ice cream van parked on offside	Unattended, no danger or children present reducing speed, taking a lower gear.
Cross roads ahead, I have priority	Open or Blind. I will take centre line position to minimise danger from the nearside.
Warning sign ahead	Bend to the offside. Check mirrors, adjust my vehicle position and approach speed to negotiate the bend watching the limit point.
School sign	Bearing in mind the time of day, day of week, month of year, are there children about?
Cattle sign	I will keep a sharp look out because animals tend to wander out in front of traffic.
Light is poor	I will use dipped headlamps to see and be seen, I will show extreme caution. Bad light affects vision including pedestrians.

Try to imagine that the person for whom you are commentating cannot see and has no idea where you are, what you are doing and why you are doing it. It is your task to outline events as they occur as fully as your speed and commitments allow, satisfying all safety aspects.

A commentary which cannot be heard is a wasted effort. Speak up, particularly when travelling at high speed when the combined noises of wind, tyre suction, engine and transmission make it difficult for you to be heard.

Commentary on the system

It is most important that you learn the five phases of the system of car control and put them into operation. Try doing this for hazards such as traffic lights, major junctions, obstructions and where you intend to turn. Now you have to fill in the spaces between systems and for this you need a good knowledge of the Highway Code.

Below are examples of this.

System of car control

I am driving the vehicle to the System of Car Control. This is a way of approaching and negotiating hazards that is methodical, safe and leaves nothing to chance. It is a systematic way of dealing with an unpredictable environment, which is potentially dangerous.

System commentary for a hazard

Ahead now I see a direction sign indicating a crossroads. I intend to turn left and travel towards Cardiff. Before each phase of the system I shall take, use and give information. Mirror, I am already in position. Mirror, I am signalling to the vehicle behind and I am adjusting my speed. Having got the correct speed I am selecting a suitable gear. I am checking my mirror again and accelerating away from the hazard.

Hazards

A hazard is anything, which is an actual or potential danger. On the road I could meet physical hazards such as junctions, variations in road surfaces or those caused by weather conditions, for example icy roads or poor visibility.

Reduction in speed limit

Ahead now I see speed restriction signs for 30 mph. I check the mirror and the speedometer and reduce the speed by acceleration sense to the maximum permitted speed as I pass the signs.

Acceleration sense

I am reducing speed by acceleration sense, which is the ability to vary vehicle speed, in response to changing road and traffic conditions, by accurate use of the accelerator.

Principles of cornering

As I negotiate the bend or corner, you will see that my vehicle is in the correct position, I am travelling at the right speed, I am in the correct gear for that speed, I am able to stop safely within the distance I can see to be clear.

Double white lines

This section of the road is controlled by a system of double white lines, with a continuous line on my side of the road. This means I must not cross or straddle it unless it is to pass something stationary in the road, to turn right in or out of premises or a junction, on the direction of a Police Officer or Traffic Warden owing to circumstances beyond my control, to avoid an accident or to pass a maintenance vehicle, pedal cycle or horse which is not travelling at more than 10 mph.

Zones

Ahead now the road disappears into a zone of invisibility. I divide the road into zones, zones of visibility, zones of invisibility, zones of safety and zones of danger. Remembering that a zone of invisibility is a potential zone of danger and I must not accelerate into these zones.

Advantages of correct steering technique

You will notice that adopting the correct steering technique provides safe and efficient steering in a wide range of circumstances which enables me to turn the wheel immediately in either direction.

The lurker

There is a large vehicle approaching; I am looking for the lurker. The fast car or motor cycle which closes up behind such vehicles and then swoops out into view.

Following position

I am moving up into a following position. By keeping at the proper distance from the vehicle in front, I will gain the following advantages. I will be able to maintain good view, which can be increased along the nearside or offside by a very slight deviation, so that I can always be aware of what is happening in the immediate vicinity.

I can stop the vehicle safely in the event of the proceeding driver braking firmly without warning.

I can extend my braking distance so that a following driver is given more time in which to react.

I can move up into an overtaking position when it is safe to do so and I will suffer less from the effects of spray from the vehicle in front.

Appendix 5: Speed and safety/feet per second

The following is a talk by Mr Justice Blair, recorded in The Listener and copied from The Journal of Criminal Law, No.5 January, 1988.

The basic cause of road accidents is widespread ignorance of ground speed, not only on the part of pedestrians but also on the part of virtually every driver of a motor car, and I add that if this widespread ignorance on the part of the road users be cured and it is curable, then there will follow a great reduction in the toll of road accidents. A speedometer does not tell anyone his ground speed. It does nothing of the kind, and it is because every motorist deludes himself into believing that a speedometer tells him how fast he is covering the ground that the danger or road accidents is increased. A speedometer gives you your speed in miles per hour. Have you any mental picture of the length of any hour or the length of a mile? No one has. How then, can anyone possibly get a mental picture of his ground speed when he is asked to put two unreliable factors together and obtain a result?

I have tried very many running down cases. Judges are conscientious when trying cases and I always felt that in order to understand any motor case it was necessary that I work out a respective speed of each vehicle in a measure that would tell me their respective ground speeds. The only measure that would give me any mental picture of the speed at which a vehicle covered the ground was the measure of feet per second. That involved me in a lot of Arithmetic. Sixty miles per hour works out at 87.9 recurring feet per second and every time I converted miles per hour into feet per second I got a result in recurring decimals. So then I had to look for a simple formula, and this is how I got it.

Instead of calling 60 mph 87 odd feet per second, I called it 90 feet per second and that gave me the simple formula of adding half to my miles per hour to obtain speed in feet per second correct within 2%. Ever since then, I have driven cars and tried running down cases in feet per second. Now what I say to all motorists is that they try doing what I do, that is always to drive and think in speed in feet per second instead of in miles per hour, and you will at once become a 100% better and safer driver. All you have to do is to add one half to the figure of your speed in mph and you will get your speed in feet per second.

Any child can do that. The other aspect of road safety touches what is called kinetic energy, which means the moving force possessed by a vehicle in motion. I can't give you a more detailed explanation but another way to put it is to refer to kinetic energy as the kick possessed by a moving vehicle. A small motor car weighing about a ton and moving at a speed of 40 miles per hour strikes the same blow as 18 ten ton steam rollers travelling at their highest speed, which is 3 mph. That is the force you are handling when you speed up a light car to 40 mph 60 feet per second. If you are driving a big seven seater two ton car at 60 mph (90 feet per second) its kinetic energy is more than that of 100 ten ton steam rollers moving at 3 mph.

Excellent advice, and as citizens we wish that every driver of a motor car would bear Mr Justice Blair's words of wisdom in mind.

Unhappily, human nature is such that when travelling from one place to another drivers are all inspired with the same desire, to get to a destination as soon as possible., so travel as fast as possible, the controls comprised by the words 'possible' being (1) regard your safety, (2) road sense, (3) consideration for others, and (4) the law.

'Feet per second' and 'kinetic energy' (see Table A5.1) do not occur to most of us, until after the accident.

Table A5.1 Justice Blair's theory

JB = 1.5 × speed = feet / meters per									
Feet per sec	Meters per sec	Speed per hour	Multiplier	Braking distance		Thinking distance		Overall stopping	
45	13.73	30	1.5	45	13.73	30	9.15	75	22.88
60	18.30	40	2	80	24.40	40	12.20	120	36.60
75	22.88	50	2.5	125	38.13	50	15.25	175	53.38
90	27.45	60	3	180	54.90	60	18.30	240	73.20
105	32.03	70	3.5	245	74.73	70	21.35	315	96.08
120	36.60	80	4	320	97.60	80	24.40	400	122.00
135	41.18	90	4.5	405	123.53	90	27.45	495	150.98
150	45.75	100	5	500	152.50	100	30.50	600	183.00
165	50.33	110	5.5	605	184.53	110	33.55	715	218.08
180	54.90	120	6	720	219.60	120	36.60	840	256.20
195	59.48	130	6.5	845	257.73	130	39.65	975	297.38
210	64.05	140	7	980	298.90	140	72.70	1120	341.60
225	68.63	150	7.5	1125	343.13	150	45.75	1275	388.88
240	73.20	160	8	1280	390.40	160	48.80	1440	439.20
255	77.78	170	8.5	1445	440.73	170	51.85	1615	492.58
270	82.35	180	9	1620	494.10	180	54.90	1800	549.00
285	86.93	190	9.5	1805	550.53	190	57.95	1995	608.48
300	91.50	200	10	2000	610.00	200	61.00	2200	671.00

Glossary

Air Amb.	Air Ambulance
ACPO	Association of Chief Police Officers
DTAG	Driver Training Advisory Group
E&U	Emergency and Utility Vehicles
EWE	Emergency Warning Equipment
HATO	Highways Agency Traffic Officers
HDS	High Dependency Service
PDC	Pre-Driving Check
PPE	Personal Protective Equipment
PTS	Patient Transport Service
RDS	Radio Data System
RTA	Road Traffic Act
RTI	Road Traffic Incident
RTR	Road Traffic Regulations
RVLR	Road Vehicle Lighting Regulations
SITREPS	Situation Reports
SRD	Solo Response Driver
SRV	Solo Response Vehicle
TSR	Traffic Sign Regulations
VDI	Vehicle Daily Inspection

References

Coyne P, Police Foundation, Mares P, MacDonald B. (2007) Roadcraft: The Essential Police Driver's Handbook. Norwich, The Stationery Office

Highway Code (2007) Available at http://www.direct.gov.uk/en/TravelAndTransport/Highwaycode/index.htm

National Centre for Policing Excellence (2007) Practice Advice on the Policing of Roads. Wyboston, National Centre for Policing Excellence and Association of Chief Police Officers

Road Traffic Act 1988

Road Vehicle Construction and Use Regulations 1986 (Reg. 99, 101 and 107)

Road Vehicle Lighting Regulations 2005 (Reg. 24)

Traffic Signs and General Direction Regulations 2002 (Regs. 33, 34, 35, 36 (1) (b))

TS&GDR Motorways 2002 (Reg. (a/b))